Harry Potter's Cookbook

Magical Collection of Culinary Wonders

Mouthwatering, Flavorful Dishes that Both Muggles and Magical Folk Alike

Can Delight Over!

Table of Contents

Introduction

We used the Harry Potter movies and books as references for ideas of the kinds of foods and drinks we thought that Muggles and Magic folk alike would be into. We then created this collection of unusual recipes that we hope you will gain much enjoyment from! We encourage you to get creative in the kitchen, and try your hand at cooking up some of these tasty meals without using any charms or potions! Combining these recipes with your magical charms is the sure ingredients to a delightful dish that is sure to please you and your meal companions to no end! Delight your taste-buds, when you try making some of these meals and desserts. Enjoy experiencing dining on similar meals that the Wizards and Witches of Hogwarts are partaking in daily in their magical world!

1. Custard Pie

Now this particular custard pie is not going to throw itself in to someone's face, unlike the ones you would get from the Weasley brothers. The bewitchment has been removed from this recipe, so you can calmly sit down to enjoy a leisurely big slice of custard pie whenever you choose to indulge in this delightful treat!

Serving Size: 6

Prep Time: 30 minutes

Ingredients:

- 1 cup all-purpose flour
- 3 eggs

- 3 tablespoons water (iced)
- ½ teaspoon salt
- 2 ½ cups hot milk
- 1 teaspoon vanilla essence
- 1 pinch nutmeg and salt
- ¾ cup sugar

Directions:

1. In a mixing bowl, add the salt and flour and mix. Cut in the shortening then use a pastry blender and mix until it is the size of peas.

2. Sprinkle one tablespoon of water over mixture and toss with a fork until flour has moistened and is beginning to pull from the side of bowl.

3. Take pastry and roll into a bowl, then place it in the fridge for 45 minutes.

4. Heat the oven to 425° Fahrenheit.

5. On a surface that is pre-dusted with flour roll out the pastry.

6. Place into a 9-inch pie dish and press down firmly to the bottom and sides of pie plate.

7. Trim the pastry 1-inch over the rim then fold it back to create a lip on top.

8. Line the entire pastry dish with a double layer of tin foil.

9. Bake for 10 minutes, then remove the foil then brown for 2 to 4 minutes.

10. Push down any bubbles that appear with the back of a spoon.

11. Whisk the eggs in a bowl, then add sugar, nutmeg, vanilla, ¼ teaspoon salt.

12. Mix well, then add the hot milk.

13. Gently pour the mixture into the pie crust.

14. Cover the edges of the pie with foil to prevent burning. Bake at 375° Fahrenheit for 25 to 30 minutes or until fully cooked.

15. Allow to cool for an hour, can serve warm or cold.

2. Sticky Toffee Pudding

This mouthwatering sponge cake based pudding is sold at the Leaky Cauldron, but you also have the choice of making it right in the comfort of your own home.

Serving Size: 6

Prep Time: 30 minutes

Ingredients:

- 2 large eggs
- 1 teaspoon vanilla essence
- 1 cup sugar
- 1 teaspoon baking soda

- 1 teaspoon baking powder
- 1 ½ cups pitted dates (chopped)
- ¼ cup unsalted butter (room temperature)
- 1 ½ cups all-purpose flour

For sauce:

- ice cream or whipped cream for serving
- 1 teaspoon brandy (optional)
- ½ teaspoon vanilla extract
- ¼ cup unsalted butter
- ½ cup heavy cream
- 1 ¼ cup brown sugar (packed)

Directions:

1. Preheat the oven to 350° Fahrenheit.

2. Lightly flour and butter a bundt cake pan.

3. In 1 ¼ cup of water boil the dates, then remove from heat.

4. Stir in the baking soda. The mixture should foam, allow it to cool.

5. Mix the salt, baking powder, and 1 ½ cups of flour in mixing bowl.

6. Beat the sugar, vanilla, and butter with an electric mixer until well blended.

7. Add 1 egg to mixture.

8. Fold half of the flour and dates into the butter mixture beat until well blended.

9. Repeat until all of the eggs, flour and dates have been added to the mix.

10. Pour the batter into the bundt cake pan.

11. Bake for about 40 to 45 minutes until the cake is fully cooked (toothpick comes clean).

12. To make the sauce, boil the butter, sugar, and cream in a saucepan, stirring constantly.

13. After about 3 minutes, remove from heat and add in the vanilla essence and brandy.

14. Cool to room temperature.

15. Slice and serve with sauce, ice cream or cream.

3. Canary Cream Puffs

These canary cream puffs will not turn people into birds, although that does sound like it would be fun! These are unlike those sold by George and Fred Weasley. They look like ordinary cream puffs, but they taste like magic!

Serving Size: 6

Prep Time: 20 minutes

Ingredients:

- 2 tablespoons water
- 1 package (500g/18 oz) cream cheese
- 1 egg yolk
- 1 box cake mix (lemon/orange)
- ¼ cup sugar
- ¼ cup walnuts (optional)

Directions:

1. Preheat the oven to 375° Fahrenheit.

2. Mix the egg yolk, water, cream cheese and cake mix by hand until dough has been formed.

3. In a small bowl mix the sugar and nuts together.

4. Form dough balls about the size of golf balls.

5. Roll the dough balls in the sugar and nuts until fully covered.

6. Place the dough balls on a greased baking sheet and bake for 10 to 12 minutes.

7. The pastries should look puffed and golden underneath.

8. If you desire serve them with cream or custard.

9. You may choose to leave out the nuts and only use sugar if you prefer.

10. If you want to try different flavors try different varieties of cake mixes.

4. Meatballs & Onion Sauce

Another yummy dish that Mrs. Weasley is famous for, many friends love to visit her when she is serving her special meatballs with onion sauce.

Serving Size: 6

Prep Time: 30 minutes

Ingredients:

- 1 can chicken soup/broth
- 1 tablespoon all-purpose flour
- 4 tablespoons olive oil
- pinch of nutmeg
- pinch of salt and pepper
- 2 tablespoons parsley (fresh chopped)
- 1 large egg
- 2 onions (chopped)
- ½ cup breadcrumbs
- 1 lb. Lean ground beef

Directions:

1. Combine in a mixing bowl the beef, egg, breadcrumbs, parsley, nutmeg, 1 onion, salt and pepper.

2. In a skillet over medium-high heat, warm half of the oil.

3. Roll the meat mixture into golf ball-sized balls and brown them in the skillet, turning them regularly until they are cooked through.

4. Add the remaining oil to a saucepan and sauté the onions until golden brown.

5. Add the flour and stir to combine with onion.

6. Pour in the chicken soup/broth and cook until mix bubbles and becomes thick.

7. Warm the meatballs and serve them with the onion sauce.

8. They can be served on a bed of rice, with mashed potato or noodles.

5. Chicken & Ham Pie

If you had of been at the Burrow, you would have likely have enjoyed a slice of Molly Weasley's chicken and ham pie. If not, no need to worry because you can easily prepare it in your own home.

Serving Size: 6

Prep Time: 45 minutes

Ingredients:

- 2 celery stalks (chopped)
- 3 medium potatoes (chopped)
- 2 onions (chopped)

- 3 medium carrots (sliced)
- 4 thin slices ham (cut into thin strips)
- 6 chicken breasts (boneless and cubed)
- 1 pack pastry dough
- salt and pepper to taste
- 1 egg (beaten)
- 1 ¼ cup milk
- 3 tablespoons plain flour
- 3 tablespoons butter
- 2 tablespoons parsley (chopped)
- 1 teaspoon thyme (dried)
- 3 ½ cups hot chicken stock
- 1 lemon (juiced)

Directions:

1. In a large saucepan, add the chicken stock, chicken, celery, potatoes, carrots, half of thyme, and some seasoning. Bring the mixture to a boil.

2. Reduce the heat to a simmer for 15 minutes.

3. Pour the mixture into a colander with a bowl under it to catch the liquid.

4. Reserve 1 pint of the stock. You can freeze the rest of it for later use if you want to.

5. In a saucepan, cook the onions in butter until they are soft. Add in flour and stock, a little at a time, until you have a thick smooth sauce.

6. Add the milk then simmer the mixture for 2 minutes, then remove it from heat.

7. Stir in the remaining parsley, thyme and lemon juice. Season to taste.

8. In an ovenproof dish mix together the vegetables, ham and chicken.

9. Pour the sauce over the top and leave to cool.

10. Preheat oven to 350° Fahrenheit.

11. Roll the pastry out and cut in a thin 1-inch strip, long enough to go around the dish.

12. Cut a circular piece of pastry that is large enough to cover the top of the dish with an extra piece for a lip.

13. Brush the rim of the dish with egg and paste the strip all the way around the rim.

14. Lift the pastry round onto the top of the dish and squeeze gently together to seal.

15. Cut off any excess pastry and brush the top of pastry with a little egg.

16. Make 4 slits in the middle of the pie and use a fork to mark all the edges.

17. Bake the pie for about 25 to 30 minutes or until the pie is golden brown.

18. Serve piping hot!

6. Trifle

This trifle is so yummy that you are going to think that you are dining at the Hogwarts's welcome feast! This is a wonderful sponge cake layered dessert that is enjoyed by muggles and wizards alike, which is served at many different occasions! Trifles were originally a seasonal pudding in many homes, but in today's world they are made with a lot of variation, but this particular recipe is a classic recipe that will delight your taste-buds to no end!

Serving Size: 10

Prep Time: 60 minutes

Ingredients:

- 4 cups water
- 2 crushed amaretto biscuits (optional)
- 1 tablespoon icing sugar
- 1 teaspoon vanilla extract
- 2 cups heavy or double cream
- 4 tablespoons sherry
- 2 Madeira cakes (cubed)
- 5 cups milk
- 5 tablespoons custard powder
- 3 tablespoons powdered gelatine (or 9 leaf gelatine)
- 1 cup caster sugar
- 3 cups frozen blueberries (blackberry, strawberry, blueberries)

Directions:

1. Add the fruit, water, and ¾ cup of sugar to a saucepan and simmer for 2 minutes.

2. Scoop out around 6 tablespoons of the fruit along with 1/8th of the juice.

3. Simmer the balance of the fruit for an additional 5 minutes.

4. Dissolve gelatin in some water.

5. Purée your cooked fruit and strain it through a sieve, leaving the skins and pits behind.

6. Add the gelatin to the thick fruit juice, and mix well and place in the fridge until almost set.

7. In a pot, make the custard using the custard powder, remaining sugar, and milk. Cook to a thick custard. Cover the mixture and allow it to cool.

8. In a trifle bowl, add the cake, the juice and the fruit that was kept along with sherry.

9. Soak the cake well, then pour the custard on top of cake and cover cake with custard.

10. Allow it to cool and set so that the jelly will not seep through.

11. Spoon jelly over the top of custard and then place in fridge until ready to finish.

12. Whip cream, icing sugar, and vanilla essence until it forms peaks.

13. Spoon over the jelly once it has completely set.

14. Sprinkle crushed biscuits over top before serving.

15. You can also add sliced almonds and other nuts as well as glacé cherries on top.

7. Crumpets

Just imagine that you can savor these yummy crumpets just like Ron and Harry, add marshmallows too if you like! The Minister of Magic and Fred Weasley also took great pleasure from these pancake-like snacks with butter and jam. These crumpets go very well with a nice cup of tea!

Serving Size: 10

Prep Time: 90 minutes

Ingredients:

- 1 teaspoon caster sugar
- 1 tablespoon yeast
- ½ cup all-purpose flour
- ½ cup white bread flour
- olive oil for cooking
- 1 teaspoon salt
- ¾ cup warm water
- ½ teaspoon bicarbonate soda
- 1 ½ cups warm milk

Directions:

1. Begin by mixing the 2 flours together in a large mixing bowl. Then add the yeast.

2. In another bowl mix the milk and sugar until well-blended. Add mixture into flour bowl mix.

3. Mix until the batter becomes nice and smooth.

4. Leave mixture covering bowl with tea towel for about one hour.

5. There should be visual evidence that the dough has risen and subsided again.

6. Add the warm water, salt and bicarbonate soda to the dough and beat it. Add the water in little bits until you have a creamy pourable mixture.

7. Heat a griddle or flat base pan. Pour small-circular amounts of mixture into pan.

8. When bubbles appear on top of crumpets turn them over.

9. Serve warm with butter, jam, honey or cream as preferred.

8. Cauldron Cakes

You do not have to wait for the lunch trolley to show up instead you can make yummy cauldron cakes yourself at home! Like most muggles, you may have to make do with using a muffin tin if you do not have mini cauldrons to bake with.

Serving Size: 20

Prep Time: 35 minutes

Ingredients:

- 1 teaspoon vanilla extract
- 1 cup milk
- ½ cup soft butter or margarine
- 1 teaspoon salt
- 3 ½ teaspoons baking powder
- 1 ½ cups sugar
- 2 cups all-purpose flour
- 3 eggs
- 1/8 teaspoon ginger
- ¾ teaspoon cinnamon

Directions:

1. Preheat oven to 350° Fahrenheit.

2. Mix butter, cinnamon, sugar, eggs, ginger, and vanilla in mixing bowl.

3. Whip mix for about 2 minutes or until well combined.

4. Mix in the solid ingredients.

5. Slowly add in the milk and make sure there are no lumps.

6. Pour mixture into greased muffin tins, filling them 2/3 of tins.

7. Bake for 25 minutes or until done.

8. Allow to cool then you can serve in a stack or on their own.

9. Add honey or perhaps frosting to them if you prefer.

9. Kreacher's French Onion Soup

Enjoy this tasty, hearty soup that Mrs. Weasley likes to serve, it is sure to warm you up while filling your tummy with this tasty soup!

Serving Size: 2

Prep Time: 30 minutes

Ingredients:

- ¼ cup red wine
- 2 ½ cups beef stock
- 2 onions

- 1 tablespoon butter
- 1 small baguette (sliced)
- 2 teaspoons canola oil
- 1/3 cup buttermilk
- pinch of sugar
- pinch of salt and pepper
- 1 bay leaf
- 1 teaspoon thyme
- 1 tablespoon plain flour
- 4 slices of Swiss cheese, shredded

Directions:

1. Slice the onions into fine slices or strips.

2. Preheat the oven to 350° Fahrenheit.

3. Add a thin layer of butter to baguettes, and then sprinkle with shredded cheese.

4. Grill baguettes until brown and crisp.

5. Add the tablespoon of butter into saucepan, melt and sauté onion strips.

6. Sprinkle onions with sugar, salt and pepper.

7. Cook onions until they become brown and caramelized.

8. Add the flour into pan by sprinkling it into pan.

9. Add beef stock and wine to pan.

10. Add the thyme and bay leaf to pan and stir.

11. Heat until the soup begins to simmer.

12. Cook for about 30 minutes on low heat.

13. Serve soup with crisp baguette croutons.

14. Sprinkle some more shredded cheese over the top of soup before serving.

10. Mulled Mead

You can get this yummy brew at Hogsmeade, Three Broomsticks Inn and the Leaky Cauldron. This is a favorite refreshment of Hagrid's and is also occasionally enjoyed by other teachers such as Cornelius Fudge, Professor Flitwick, Professor McGonagall, and even the Minister of Magic himself.

Serving Size: 4

Prep Time: 15 Minutes

Ingredients:

- 3 tablespoons brandy
- 1 piece fresh ginger (about 5 cm)
- 3 cloves
- 1 cinnamon stick
- 1 lemon peel (small strip)
- 8 ½ fluid ounces of apple juice
- 25 fluid ounces of cider or mead

Directions:

1. Pour the mead or cider into a medium saucepan.

2. Carefully add the lemon peel, brandy and apple juice. Stir gently.

3. Add in the sliced ginger, cloves and cinnamon stick.

4. Warm mixture until it begins to simmer then remove all of the spices from pan.

5. Pour fluid through a mesh into serving glasses for a warming, festive drink that you are sure to enjoy!

11. Mince Pies

You can enjoy the mince pies just like the ones that dear Mrs. Weasley sent to Harry for Christmas. These traditional mince pies are filled with a fruity and sweet flavor for a seasonal feast.

Serving Size: 12 to 16

Prep Time: 15 minutes

Ingredients:

- 2 cups all-purpose flour
- 1 cup butter or margarine (for baking)

- ½ an ounce vinegar
- ½ teaspoon salt
- 8 teaspoons ice water
- 1 teaspoon caster sugar (for dusting)
- 4 cups minced fruit
- 1 egg yolk (keep white for brushing)

Instructions:

1. Mix the salt, margarine, and flour in a food processor.

2. Beat the egg yolk, water, and vinegar. Then add mixture to dry ingredients.

3. Once you have a nice firm dough wrap it up in cling wrap and place in the fridge for an hour.

4. Preheat the oven to 430° Fahrenheit.

5. Roll dough out thinly then cut the dough into rounds about 10 cm in diameter.

6. Place rounds into a greased muffin pan.

7. Fill each round with some of the minced fruit.

8. Now dampen the edges of the pastry, adding the 7 cm round on top.

9. To seal pastry gently seal the edges together.

10. To allow steam to escape prick some holes on the top of pies.

11. Brush tops slightly with the egg whites and then place them into the oven for about 10-15 minutes.

12. Once pies are golden brown in color remove them from the oven and sprinkle the tops with caster sugar while still hot.

13. Allow pies to cool then serve them as part of your festive feast!

12. Christmas Pudding

At the traditional Hogwarts Christmas feast there is Christmas pudding, or plum pudding served, and it is often set alight and served as a flaming pudding which has been soaked in brandy, although not to the young wizards. This is a yummy treat that can be enjoyed any time of year, but it is usually eaten with Christmas lunch.

Serving Size: 2 large puddings

Prep Time: 8 hours

Ingredients:

- 7 ounces candied citrus peel
- 1 ounce blanched almonds
- 2 large cooking apples
- 2 tablespoons of brandy
- 3 large eggs
- 3 ½ ounces light sugar
- 4 ounces plain flour
- 3 ½ ounces soft breadcrumbs
- 2 pounds raisins
- 1 tablespoon nutmeg

For the ginger butter:

- 4 tablespoons brandy
- ½ orange zested
- 5 tablespoons icing sugar
- 6 ounces butter, unsalted
- 2 stems ginger (chopped fine)

Directions:

1. Core and peel the apples, and chop them into small pieces.

2. Chop the candied peel into small pieces.

3. Also chop the blanched almonds into small pieces.

4. Mix in a mixing bowl all of the pudding ingredients, except the butter.

5. Grate the butter into the mixture, about ¼ of the quantity at a time. Each time stirring into the mix.

6. Butter 2 large pudding bowls and line them with greaseproof paper.

7. Scrape the pudding mix into both bowls and cover with the greaseproof paper, allowing a little space for expansion and tie with piece of string.

8. Make a watertight seal using foil wrapping the package from above and below.

9. In a saucepan stream or boil the pudding for about 8 hours, replacing water as needed.

10. Remove the pudding from the saucepan and allow it to cool overnight.

11. Remove the wrappings, and replace them with new wrappings and store the pudding in a cool, dry place.

12. For the brandy butter, cream the sugar, orange zest and butter together.

13. Beat in the chopped ginger and brandy. Place the bowl in the fridge to set.

14. You can freeze the butter up to 40 days or store in the fridge for a little while.

15. When you are ready to serve the pudding boil it for an hour, then unwrap and take it out.

16. Pour a few teaspoons of brandy over the pudding and set it on fire.

13. Christmas Cake

This is a traditional fruitcake that is enjoyed in many parts of the world over the Christmas season, but is good to eat any time of the year. During the Hogwarts Christmas feast the students enjoy Christmas cake. One of the great Christmas cake makers was Molly Weasley, although in this particular recipe we do not include the toy penguin.

Serving Size: 10

Prep Time: 3 hours

Ingredients:

- 2 lbs. Mixed dried fruit of your choice
- 3 ½ ounces almonds (or other nuts)
- 2 teaspoons vanilla extract
- 2 teaspoons mixed spice
- 4 eggs
- 7 1/2 ounces plain flour
- 8 ounces brown sugar
- 8 ounces unsalted butter (softened)
- 2 oranges or lemons (zest and juice)
- 5 ounces sherry, rum, brewed tea or brandy

Directions:

1. In a mixing bowl, add fruit and alcohol/tea, along with lemon juice and lemon zest. Let this mixture stand overnight.

2. Heat the oven to 32o° Fahrenheit.

3. Butter and line a cake tin with enough baking paper that will stick out above the tin about 2.5 cm then wrap the entire tin with some paper, secured with string or staples.

4. Beat the vanilla, butter, and sugar until creamy.

5. Add the spice, flour, soaked fruit along with liquid and nuts.

6. Mix the butter and fruit mix together then scrape it into the cake tin.

7. Using a spoon make a dent in the middle of the cake.

8. Bake for 1 ½ hours.

9. Reduce the heat to 285° Fahrenheit and cover the cake with tin foil.

10. Bake the cake for about 45 minutes to 1 hour or until a knife comes out clean when poked in the middle of the cake.

11. Cool the cake in the tin.

12. Lift the cake out of the tin and cover it with greaseproof paper.

13. Keep cake in sealed container for 6 months, opening every two weeks to poke and add a little alcohol or tea that you choose.

14. Serve cake with custard or on its own after 6 months or longer.

14. Cornish Pasties

You can enjoy delicious Cornish pasties served at the Three Broomsticks Inn, that are made up of meat, vegetables and potato in a pastry wrapping. During the Triwizard Tournament these were served for lunch on the day of the 3rd task. Enjoy this tasty dish in the comfort of your own home for lunch or dinner!

Serving Size: 6

Prep Time: 1 hour 10 minutes

Ingredients:

- 1 teaspoon salt
- 4 ounces unsalted butter

- 2 teaspoons baking powder
- 3 ½ cups plain flour
- salt and pepper to taste
- 1 egg (beaten, for brushing)
- 3 tablespoons butter
- 1 tablespoon plain flour for dusting
- 10 ounces beef (minced or finely chopped)
- 5 ounces mixed vegetables (finely chopped)
- 5 ounces onion (finely chopped)
- 3 ½ cups potato (finely chopped)
- 125 grams cold water
- 2 egg yolks

Directions:

1. Add to food processor baking powder, flour, salt, egg yolks, and butter and blitz until the mixture becomes crumbly.

2. Add water until the crumbly mixture becomes a dough. You may not need all the water.

3. In a cling-film wrap the dough and leave in the fridge to chill for an hour.

4. You can partially cook the filling ingredients beforehand or use them as is.

5. Preheat the oven to 350° Fahrenheit.

6. In the rolled out pastry cut six circles, about the size of dinner plates.

7. Mix the beef in a bowl along with 1 tablespoon of flour and salt and pepper.

8. Season with vegetables.

9. Add the beef and vegetables to the pastry, filling one half, but leaving a lip for closure.

10. Place little amounts of butter on the beef and vegetables and then brush edges with egg.

11. Fold over the other half and crimp the edges to seal the pastry completely.

12. Brush with egg then add small slit in top of pastry to allow steam to escape.

13. Bake in the oven for 40 to 50 minutes until the pastry becomes golden brown and the meat and vegetables are fully cooked.

14. Allow the pie to cool and serve on its own or with a garden salad.

15. Bath Buns

This is a rich, sweet pastry with crunchy sugar on top that Hagrid offered to Harry and Ron, but they couldn't accept his version. This version I am glad to say is much more palatable.

Serving Size: 6

Prep Time: 60 Minutes

Ingredients:

- 3 ½ cups plain flour
- 3 tablespoons sugar cubes (coarsely crushed)
- 4 tablespoons cut citrus peel
- 6 ounces raisins or sultanas
- 3 eggs
- 4 tablespoons butter
- 11 ounces warm water
- 10 ounces warm milk
- 1 teaspoon salt
- 2 teaspoons dried yeast
- 6 tablespoons caster sugar

Directions:

1. Add about 1 ½ cups flour, yeast, 1 teaspoon caster sugar, warm milk and water into mixing bowl. Beat with a wooden spoon until mixture is well combined.

2. Allow to stand in warm area for about 20 minutes or until frothy.

3. In another bowl, add the rest of the flour, and rub in the butter until it becomes crumbly. Add in the previously made mixture.

4. Add in 2 beaten eggs, 6 tablespoons caster sugar, the fruit, and the citrus peel.

5. Beat the mixture well and leave it to stand, covered with a damp tea towel for about 1 ½ hours.

6. Preheat the oven to 425° Fahrenheit, and grease a baking sheet.

7. Place tablespoons of dough onto the greased baking sheet, leaving space between them.

8. Allow them to stand in a warm place for about 30 minutes, covered with oiled cling-wrap or plastic lid.

9. Beat the remaining egg, 1 teaspoon caster sugar, and 1 tablespoon of water together until well combined to make the glaze.

10. Uncover the buns and brush them with the glaze mixture and sprinkle tops with coarse sugar.

11. Bake the buns for about 15 to 20 minutes or until they are golden brown.

12. Place buns on a wire rack to cool.

13. You can exchange the raisins for other dried fruit if you wish.

16. Rock Cakes

For most of the magic folks at Hogwarts Hagrid's rock cakes were a little too rock-like. The recipe below is a less rocky version of these delicious fruitcakes.

Serving Size: 6

Prep Time: 30 Minutes

Ingredients:

- 8 ounces self-raising flour
- 2 teaspoons vanilla essence
- 1 egg
- 5 ½ ounces dried fruit of your choice

- 4 ½ ounces unsalted butter (cubed)
- 1 tablespoon milk
- 2 ½ ounces caster sugar
- 1 teaspoon baking powder

Directions:

1. Preheat the oven to 350° Fahrenheit.

2. Line a baking tray with parchment or baking paper.

3. Beat the milk, vanilla essence and egg in a mixing bowl.

4. Mix all of the dry ingredients in a bowl.

5. Add the wet ingredients to the dry ingredients and combine well.

6. This should leave you with a thick, lumpy looking dough.

7. If the dough is too dry, add one tablespoon of milk at a time until you reach the desired consistency.

8. Spoon a golf-ball size lump onto the baking tray, making sure there is enough room for the dough to flatten and spread out while baking.

9. Bake for about 15 to 20 minutes or until the cake turns to a nice golden brown color.

10. Remove from the oven and allow them to cool for a few minutes.

11. Place them onto a wire rack to cool.

12. Serve with tea at any time. These cakes will keep for about a week in a sealed container.

17. Spotted Dick & Custard

Another favorite feast is spotted dick! It is a suet pudding, steamed, and is usually filled with currants, raisins, or other fruit and is served with custard, this yummy tasty dessert tastes much better than its name sounds. The Hogwarts house-elves make a version of this that even Hermione cannot resist.

Serving Size: 6

Prep Time: 2 hours

Ingredients:

- 75 fluid ounces heavy cream
- 6 egg yolks

- 1 teaspoon butter (for greasing)
- 14 fluid ounces milk
- 1 lemon (zested)
- 4 ounces raisins, or currants
- 5 ounces caster sugar
- 5 ounces suet, shredded
- 2 teaspoon baking powder
- 10 ounces plain flour

Directions:

1. Mix the flour, suet, ½ of the caster sugar, lemon zest, baking powder, and currants in a mixing bowl, and combine well.

2. Add half of the milk and mix to create a soft dough.

3. Grease pudding basin with the butter and use a wooden spoon to empty the dough into the basin. Cover with greaseproof paper.

4. Tie the paper down with some string, lay a dampened tea towel over the top and secure it with more string.

5. Use a large saucepan to put the pudding basin into and fill 2/3 of the saucepan with water.

6. Place the lid on the saucepan and bring to a boil.

7. Turn down the heat and simmer for one hour.

8. Using another saucepan, bring the cream along with the rest of the milk to a simmer.

9. Whisk together the egg yolks and the rest of the caster sugar until frothy and light.

10. Pour the cream mixture and hot milk slowly into egg mixture, stirring constantly.

11. Pour the custard mix back into the saucepan and cook for a while on low heat until it thickens.

12. Slice the cooked spotted dick into 6 wedges and serve with the hot custard.

18. Smoked Kippers & Eggs

This dish is served as part of breakfast, along with eggs, toast, porridge, and bacon in the Great Hall, this was a fishy treat that was often prepared by the house-elves of Hogwarts for the enjoyment of the teachers and students alike.

Serving Size: 2

Prep Time: 25 Minutes

Ingredients:

- ½ lemon (in wedges)

- ½ cup of milk
- 1 teaspoon curry powder
- 2 tablespoons butter
- 2 kipper herrings (filleted)
- 4 large eggs (beaten)
- 4 slices whole-wheat toast
- salt and pepper to taste

Directions:

1. Melt half of the butter in a pan.

2. Fry the kippers for about 5 minutes per side, until they are firm and cooked.

3. Whisk milk, eggs, curry powder, salt and pepper, and add the remaining butter in bowl.

4. Scramble the eggs in a pan on low heat until they are nice and fluffy and light.

5. Serve the kippers and eggs with 2 slices of toast per person and squeeze lemon on top to finish off the fish.

19. Black Pudding

To enjoy this traditional British sausage, you do not need to be at the Triwizard Championship to do so. It is served at breakfast or dinner, it is a delicacy that is also enjoyed in Canada as well as Britain.

Serving Size: 10

Prep Time: 1 hour

Ingredients:

- 1 onion (yellow, large, chopped)
- 1 cup milk

- 1 teaspoon allspice (ground)
- 1 ½ teaspoons pepper
- 1 ½ cups steel-cut oatmeal
- 2 ½ teaspoons salt
- 4 cups pigs' blood (fresh)
- 2 cups pork fat (finely diced)

Directions:

1. Preheat your oven to 325° Fahrenheit.

2. Grease 2 glass loaf pans (or line 2 metal loaf pans with parchment paper)

3. Stir in 1 teaspoon of salt to the fresh pig's blood.

4. Boil 2 ½ cups of water and add in the oats.

5. Cook the oats until tender, not too soft, cook for about 15 minutes.

6. Sieve the blood to remove any lumps, then stir in the salt and pepper, allspice, milk, fat, and onion.

7. Pour evenly into the 2 pans, cover the tin with foil and bake for 1 hour or until firm.

8. Allow to cool completely.

9. Wrap in cling-wrap and freeze for longterm use or store in the fridge up to a week.

10. To serve, slice a piece about the same thickness as a slice of bread. Fry in a pan until the edges become browned and crisp. Eat with breakfast or a salad.

20. Yorkshire Pudding

The legendary Yorkshire pudding is what completes any dinner feast. At Hogwarts welcoming feast Yorkshire pudding was served. This dish is served with many meals that feature gravy and roasts. Enjoy this tasty savory extra with lunch or dinner to help soak up the sauce that is served with your meal!

Serving Size: 4

Prep Time: 10 Minutes

Ingredients:

- 2 tablespoons melted butter
- 3 eggs (beaten)

- ½ teaspoon salt
- ¾ cup cake flour
- 7 fluid ounces milk
- 3 tablespoons cooking oil

Directions:

1. Preheat oven to 375° Fahrenheit.

2. Place 1 teaspoon of oil into the bottom of each muffin form in a muffin tin with 8 molds.

3. Place in the oven until the oil starts to sizzle.

4. In a mixing bowl, sift flour and salt.

5. Stir in the melted butter and eggs.

6. Whisk the milk into the mixture until smooth.

7. Pour mixture into the prepared muffin tin.

8. Bake for about 25 minutes, then remove it from oven.

9. Turn the oven down to 320° Fahrenheit and prick puddings with toothpick.

10. Put back into oven for 5 more minutes.

11. Allow them to cool slightly, then serve them with roast and gravy.

12. May want to warm in oven before serving.

21. Steak & Kidney Pie

The house-elves of Hogwarts take great delight in both eating and making tasty steak and kidney pies. Steak and kidney pies are traditionally made from beef that is chopped into pieces along with lamb kidney in a thick pastry. This is a dish that is hearty and is well suited for winter weather.

Serving Size: 6

Prep Time: 3 hours

Ingredients:

- 1.7 lbs. Cubed beef, minimal fat content
- 3 teaspoons vegetable oil
- 1 egg (for brushing)

- 1 onion (large, chopped)
- ½ lb. Lamb or ox kidney
- 2 teaspoons lemon juice
- 1.7 fluid ounces ice water
- 3 ½ ounces butter or margarine
- 5 ounces cake flour
- 8 ½ fluid ounces meat stock
- 1 bay leaf
- 3 tablespoons parsley (chopped)
- a pinch of black pepper
- 2 teaspoons salt

Directions:

1. Chop the beef into small cubes, about an inch on each edge.

2. Soak the kidney in salty lukewarm water.

3. Slice the kidney in half, remove the inner core and membrane. Cube the rest of it.

4. Fry the kidneys and beef cubes in a bit of oil, then add pepper and onions and sauté.

5. Add the pepper, salt and bay leaf.

6. Add the meat stock, simmer until the meat is tender for about 2 hours.

7. Once the meat has become tender, add some small amounts of flour to mix until gravy becomes thickened.

8. Allow the meat to cool while you prepare the pastry.

9. Heat the oven to 395° Fahrenheit.

10. Sift the remaining dry ingredients together.

11. Add in the butter nice and slow, then add the lemon juice and ice water until the dough is firm.

12. Pour the meat into a pastry dish and cover it with the pastry dough.

13. Put a slit at the top to allow steam to escape.

14. Brush the egg onto pastry and bake for 15 minutes or until golden brown.

22. Treacle Tart

One of Harry's favorite desserts is the treacle tart, which is mentioned numerous times. Treacle tarts are a very common British food that has been mentioned in the Voyages of Dr. Doolittle and Alice in Wonderland.

Serving Size: 4 to 8

Prep Time: 45 minutes

Ingredients:

- 2 tablespoons lemon juice
- ¼ cup heavy cream
- 1 cup golden syrup
- 1 lemon for zest

- 1 cup breadcrumbs
- 1 pack premade pie crust pastry

Directions:

1. Preheat oven to 375° Fahrenheit.

2. Shape the pastry to fit a 9-inch pie pan and spread evenly across the bottom of the plate.

3. Mix the cream, breadcrumbs, syrup, lemon zest, and lemon juice in a mixing bowl. Then pour mixture into pie plate.

4. Spread evenly over the dough.

5. Add thin strips of pastry over the top in an open mesh pattern.

6. Bake until the filling has set about 40 minutes.

7. Cool slightly then serve with ice cream or fresh whipped cream.

23. Knickerbocker Glory

You can enjoy a yummy Knickerbocker Glory without attending Dudley Dursley's birthday party. This is a version of this recipe that you will soon discover to be a yummy ice-cream treat.

Serving Size: 2

Prep Time: 10 minutes

Ingredients:

- 1 cup whipped or clotted cream

- 1 cup vanilla ice cream
- 1 cup mixed fruits chopped (peaches, strawberries, bananas and grapes)
- 1 ice cream wafer
- 1 tablespoon crushed hazelnuts
- 2 cherries
- 2 tablespoons fruit syrup

Directions:

1. Get to large milkshake glasses and use them to put Knickerbocker glory in.

2. Add some chopped fruit to base of each, to about halfway up glass.

3. Add 2 scoops of vanilla ice-cream on top of the fruit.

4. Drizzle the fruit syrup over the ice-cream in the glasses.

5. Fill the rest of the glasses with whipped cream.

6. Sprinkle with nuts on top of cream. Add the cherries and wafer to top.

7. You can change this recipe by using fruit liqueur instead of fruit syrup.

24. Pumpkin Pasty

Can you imagine yourself sitting on the Hogwarts Express
and trying such tasty treats on the Honey dukes Express food
trolley? I am sure you will enjoy this pumpkin pasty recipe
just as much as Harry and Ron did on their first trip to
Hogwarts.

Serving Size: 2

Prep Time: 30 Minutes

Ingredients:

- ¼ cup white sugar
- 8 ounces butter
- 2 tablespoons caster sugar
- ½ teaspoon salt
- 2 ½ cups flour
- ¾ cup ice water
- 1 cup fresh or tinned pumpkin purée.

Directions:

For the Pastry Crust:

1. Mix the caster sugar, salt, butter, flour, and ice water together.

2. If the mix is too wet, add small amounts of flour until the dough becomes pliable.

3. If the mix is too dry add another tablespoon of ice water at a time until the texture is reached.

4. Knead the dough into a ball, wrap it up in cling-wrap, and place into fridge for an hour.

For the Filling:

5. Mix the puréed pumpkin, pumpkin spice, and white sugar together, combine well.

6. Preheat the oven to 400° Fahrenheit.

7. Roll out the dough to about 1/8 inch thick.

8. Use a cookie cutter or cup to cut out rounds.

9. Scoop some mixture onto cutouts, place one cut out on top of other, with mixture in the middle.

10. Make a few slices across the top to allow for ventilation and crimp edges together to seal the pasties.

11. Bake on a baking tray in the oven for about 25 minutes or until golden brown.

12. Can sprinkle with a dusting of brown sugar or cinnamon for decoration before serving these tasty treats!

25. Butterbeer

Butterbeer is known as a foaming mug that is filled with a soothing, refreshing and comforting fizzy treat. The author J.K. Rowling describes the slightly sickly variation of butterscotch, as addicting. It is an amazing fizzy and delicious treat! The recipe is geared for minors, so the addition of alcoholic beverage was removed.

Serving Size: 4 beer mugs

Prep Time: 30 minutes

Ingredients:

- 32 ounces cream soda
- whipped cream
- ¼ cup butterscotch syrup
- 1 quart vanilla or butter trickle ice cream

Directions:

1. Place mugs in freezer for about 20 minutes.

2. While the glasses are chilling, place the cream soda, butterscotch syrup, ice-cream into a blender, pulsing until well-blended.

3. Divide the mixture into the frosted glasses. Top with whipped cream prior to serving.

26. Chocolate Frogs

You might think that chocolate frogs do not look too appetizing, but Chocolate Frogs were certainly part of Harry's first experiences of the wizarding world. That makes them very significant, indeed. You should be able to enjoy them as they are not really frogs but are yummy lumps of chocolate shaped to look like frogs.

Serving Size: 10-120 frogs, depending on your mold size

Prep Time: 55 minutes

Ingredients:

- 1 ½ cups milk
- dash of salt
- 2 teaspoons vanilla
- 2 cups cocoa powder
- ¾ cup sugar
- 1/3 cup milk
- 8 tablespoons gelatin powder

Directions:

1. Whisk the gelatin powder and 1/3 cup milk together then set aside.

2. In a saucepan, mix 1 ½ cups milk, salt, sugar, and cocoa powder. Mix until dissolved.

3. Heat the mixture over medium-high heat, stirring occasionally until it begins to bubble around the edges.

4. Turn off the heat before adding the gelatin mixture and vanilla essence. Stir until dissolved.

5. Rest the mixture for about 5 minutes before poring it into your frog molds. Place in the freezer for about 30 minutes until the chocolate frogs firm up.

27. Acid Pops

If you would like to try making some playful Acid Pops like the ones sold at Honeydukes in Hogsmeade village, then you can make them using my quick and easy recipe. All you will need is some colorful lollies of assorted flavors, popping candies, sour candies, and some honey to use to glue them all together!

Serving Size: 10-12 Acid Pops

Prep Time: 10 Minutes

Ingredients:

- 10 pieces sour candy, crushed
- 16.6 ounce pack flavored lollipops
- ½ cup honey
- 3 packs popping candy

Directions:

1. In separate bowls place the crushed sour candies and popping candies. Set aside.

2. Peel off covers of each lollipop, dip lightly in honey, then roll in crushed sour candies, then another dip in honey, before coating with popping candy.

3. Popping candies will lose their magic pops if exposed for too long, cover the lollies in wax paper if you are not going to serve them immediately.

28. Candied Pineapple

Do you remember Professor Slughorn? In the sixth book installment, Harry Potter and the Half-Blood Prince he was the Defense Against the Dark Arts Teacher. One of his favorite treats was Candied Pineapple. This recipe has a deep British background as a local dish.

Serving Size: 20 servings

Prep Time: 55 Minutes

Ingredients:

- ¼ cup light corn syrup
- 2 ½ cups plus ½ cup sugar

- 2 20-ounce cans sliced pineapples in heavy syrup

Directions:

1. Drain the pineapple slices and reserve 1 ½ cups of its heavy syrup.

2. In a saucepan over medium-high heat, combine the 2 1/1 cups sugar, heavy syrup, and light corn syrup. Bring to a boil for about 4 minutes, stirring continuously until the sugar dissolves.

3. Before adding the pineapple slices turn the heat to low. Turn the pineapple slices often to coat with the syrup.

4. Keep the heat on low and simmer pineapple slices for about 45 minutes or until the pineapples become translucent.

5. After cooking is completed, remove the pineapples from the pan and allow them to dry on a wire rack overnight. You may shorten this process by baking the pineapple slices at 200° Fahrenheit for 30 minutes.

6. When the pineapple slices cool completely, roll into granulated sugar to coat. Serve or store in an airtight container.

29. Homemade Toffee

At the Harry Potter and the Goblet of Fire, dear Mrs. Weasley sent everyone some homemade toffee enclosed in a pack of Easter eggs. The toffee is apparently not too difficult to recreate, nor is handling toffee for the recipe. Combining some patience and some magical kitchen skills, I am sure that you can make some yummy homemade toffee for everyone to enjoy.

Serving Size: 3 cups bite-size English Toffee

Prep Time: 40 Minutes

Ingredients:

1. Preheat oven to 425° Fahrenheit.

2. Grease a baking sheet with some cooking spray before placing the almonds down to roast in the oven for 10 minutes. Stir them halfway through baking time to avoid them from burning on one side.

3. Allow the almonds to cool a little bit before chopping them into halves or quarters.

4. Use another lightly greased baking tray to spread the chopped almonds evenly on. Set aside.

5. Heat a saucepan over medium-high heat and stir in the sugar, butter, vanilla, salt and mix constantly with a wooden spoon until it comes to a gentle boil.

6. Reduce the heat to low and simmer the mixture until it is lighter shade of the roasted almonds.

7. Spread mixture over the chopped almonds and allow it to cool and set completely.

8. In your microwave oven melt milk chocolate pieces.

9. Pour the melted chocolate over the almonds and candy, then sprinkle with crushed pecans.

10. Place the toffee in the fridge to harden before breaking it up into bite-size pieces.

30. Corned Beef Sandwich

Since the very first book, Mrs. Weasley's delightful cooking has been praised. Poor Harry lived off canned soups back in Privet Drive, so he was amazed just by the mere mention of a corned beef sandwich, Ron on the other hand did not seem so happy. Ron doesn't like corn beef, and for another he fancies the goodies sold in the food trolly more—mostly due to the fact that his family cannot afford them. He was certainly more than happy to exchange his sandwich for the goodies that his newfound friend Harry bought.

Serving Size: 4 sandwiches

Prep Time: 20 minutes

Ingredients:

- 4 tablespoons butter
- Dijon mustard
- 1 medium onion, sliced finely
- 8 ounces Fontina cheese
- 1 lb. Corned beef, finely sliced
- 8 pcs. Sliced bread

Directions:

1. To prepare the sandwich, first spread some Dijon mustard on one side of the bread. Top with corned beef, onion slices, and cheese. Repeat with the remaining 3 sandwiches.

2. In a pan over low heat, melt butter then, grill the sandwiches, for about 3 minutes per side.

3. Cut into triangles before serving.

31. Lamb Chops

Among the good foods mentioned in this book, Lamb Chops is one of the most elaborate and remarkable dishes that is a favorite to serve at family gatherings and special occasions. Most of the feasts in Harry Potter serve this recipe, offering the students a yummy mouthwatering treat with a celebratory feel.

Serving Size: 4 Servings

Prep Time: 20 Minutes

Ingredients:

- salt and pepper to taste
- 3 tablespoons water
- 2 tablespoons fresh lemon juice
- pinch of crushed red pepper
- 2 tablespoons parsley, minced
- 10 small garlic cloves, halved
- pinch dried thyme
- 3 tablespoons extra virgin olive oil
- 2 lbs. Lamb loin chops, fats trimmed

Directions:

1. Season the lamb with thyme, salt, and pepper.

2. Heat the olive oil in a skillet over medium-high heat until it is simmering.

3. Add the lamb chops and garlic halves, cooking until browned, about 3 minutes per side.

4. Transfer the chops in a serving dish, leaving the garlic in the pan.

5. Stir in the lemon juice, water, red pepper, and parsley. Allow it to sizzle for about a minute. Pour it over the cooked lamb.

32. Roast Beef

In the British cuisine roast beef is known as a staple. It was featured many times in the Harry Potter book, served mostly at extravagant feasts alongside Yorkshire Pudding. This roast beef recipe will give you a little peek into the kinds of meals that the Hogwarts students were dining on.

Serving Size: 4 Steak Servings

Prep Time: 1 hour and 15 minutes

Ingredients:

- 1 lb. Carrots, halved lengthwise
- 1 medium onion, cut into wedges

- ½ teaspoon mustard powder
- 1 teaspoon flour
- 2 lbs. Beef, top rump joint
- For the Gravy:
- 1 ½ cups beef stock
- 1 tablespoon flour

Directions:

1. Preheat the oven to 400° Fahrenheit.

2. Combine the mustard powder and flour and rub onto beef.

3. Place the carrots and onion wedges on a roasting tin such as a bed for the beef.

4. Place the beef on top and cook for 20 minutes.

5. Reduce the temperature to oven to 325° Fahrenheit, and roast the beef for another 30 minutes if you like it raw, 40 minutes if you want it medium, and about one hour if you like your meat well done.

6. Transfer the roast beef and carrots into a serving dish, set the meat drippings and onions aside. Cover the dish with a

piece of aluminum foil to keep warm. Rest the meat for about 30 minutes before serving.

7. While you are waiting for the meat to be ready, mix the remnants of the roast beef with flour, and stir until lumps disappear in a large saucepan over medium-high heat. Slowly add the beef stock to pan and stir until it begins to bubble. Season and serve with roast beef and carrots.

33. Exploding Bonbons

Honeydukes, the famous sweet shop located at the Hogsmeade Village, offered many sweet treats such as Exploding Bonbons. These were a favorite among humor lovers Fred and George Weasley as they were always assured of a good laugh from Exploding Bonbons.

Serving Size: 12 truffles

Prep Time: 3 hours and 25 Minutes

Ingredients:

- 12 ounces chocolate candy coating
- 5 packets popping candy
- 4 ounces heavy cream
- 6 ounces bittersweet chocolate chips

Directions:

1. In a small saucepan simmer the cream over medium-high heat.

2. Transfer the hot cream to a larger bowl with the chocolate chips, stirring until mixture is smooth.

3. Cover the bowl with plastic wrap, then chill it for 3 hours.

4. Scoop the chocolate ganache in a baking sheet lined with aluminum foil to form ¾-inch balls.

5. Pop the baking sheet into your freezer for about 10 minutes while you prepare the chocolate candy coating dip according to package directions.

6. Once ready, dip the popping candy coated chocolate balls on the chocolate candy coating until fully covered. Sprinkle

the bonbons with more popping candies for garnish as well as a bit of a bang!

34. Chocolate Gateau

This is a recipe that has been mentioned in among the Harry Potter pages that manages to stick. The author (Rowling) surely must have had a fondness for chocolates, as just the mention of chocolate made it something wonderful to look forward to. Rowling used it not just as comfort food but also to help ward off the ill effects of the presence of dementors. This rich chocolaty recipe will surely delight your taste-buds, along with it melt-in-your-mouth goodness of salted caramel and chocolate frosting.

Serving Size: 8-10 Servings

Prep Time: 1 hour

Ingredients:

- 12 tablespoons butter, softened
- 1 ¼ cups flour
- ¾ cup sour cream
- 2 teaspoons vanilla extract
- 2 egg yolks
- 4 eggs
- 1 ¾ cup sugar
- ¼ cup cocoa powder
- 4 ounces unsweetened chocolate
- ¾ cup hot water
- 1 teaspoon salt
- ½ teaspoon baking soda
- ½ cup almond flour
- 2 cups bittersweet chocolate frosting

Directions:

1. Preheat your oven to 350° Fahrenheit. Prepare 3 8-inch cake pans, greased with oil. Set aside.

2. Combine some hot water, cocoa powder, chocolate, in a heatproof mixing bowl.

3. Place the bowl in bain-marie, stirring the mixture until well-blended.

4. Stir in sugar into mixing bowl. Set aside.

5. Mix flour, salt, almond flour, baking powder, and baking soda.

6. Get another bowl and whisk eggs and egg yolks together. Add in the remaining sugar, mixing until creamy.

7. Stir in the chocolate mixture and mix until well-blended.

8. Slowly fold in flour mixture, sour cream, and vanilla extract, mixing until ingredients are well-blended.

9. Divide the batter between the 3 cake pans, spreading evenly.

10. Bake for 30 minutes or until toothpick comes clean. Let cool on a wire rack.

11. Use the bittersweet chocolate icing to frost the cake.

35. Pumpkin Juice

The characters of the Harry Potter book would pour themselves a glass of pumpkin juice when they just wanted to chill and relax. With my recipe, butternut squash is used to make the juice. It is then mixed together with a few other goodies to give it a delectable finish.

Serving Size: 2 Servings

Prep Time: 10 Minutes

Ingredients:

- 1 inch piece of ginger, skinned
- 1 lemon
- 1 red apple, cored
- 1 cup butternut squash slices

Directions:

1. Use a juicer to juice all of the ingredients together.

2. Strain the juice through a fine mesh then discard the solids.

3. Transfer the juice into serving glasses with ice cubes.

Conclusion

I hope that all of you die-hard Harry Potter fans will get a chance to try as many of these tasty recipes during your own special feasts that would normally only see being eaten during special occasions at Hogwarts. At the very least you will hopefully get to experience a few of the same treats that Harry, Hermione, and Ron enjoyed during the Harry Potter series.

Most of the collection is based upon traditional British cuisine that are filled with hearty fillings. Now you can use this collection of recipes to dine the same way the Wizard and Witches of Hogwarts do!

These magical tasting recipes will hopefully have your taste-buds dancing without the use of any spells or potions! Instead just the use of some wonderfully magic tasting treats that will make you feel like you are tasting a little piece of heaven here on earth!

Made in the USA
Middletown, DE
11 December 2019

80508402R00062